iPhone 6 and iPhone 6+

A Simple Guide to iPhone 6's Best Features

5 mn Smarts

Contents

iPhone 6 and iPhone 6+

What differentiates the new iPhone 6 with iOS 8? There's a long list of features that make the new iPhone improved, better, faster, and stronger, but which are the greatest features that meet your needs – Here they are:

Improved camera focus

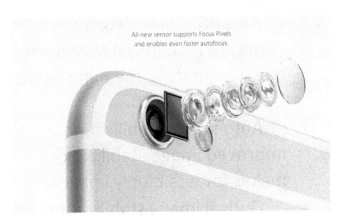

All-new sensor supports Focus Pixels and enables even faster autofocus.

In today's world, people take more photos with their iPhone than any other camera. Innovative technology has made iSight, iPhone's camera, even better with:

- Focus Pixels: The camera can now sense more information about your image, meaning it delivers a better and faster autofocus.

- Advanced face detection: Faces are recognized fasted and more accurately, meaning better face shots.

- Auto image stabilization: Improved image stabilization makes for less blurry images.

- Optical image stabilization: In short, this means better photos in low-light.

Exposure control: On-screen slider allows the user to lighten or darken images in the preview pane easily.

Bigger screen, better design

The iPhone 6 and 6 Plus have the largest screens and are the thinnest phones from Apple. However, they were designed to not feel bulky.

- Bigger size: The iPhone 6 features a 4.7 inch retina HD display screen and is 6.9mm thin and the 6 Plus a 5.5 inch retina HD display screen and is 7.1mm thin.

- Improved design: While Apple has always been sleek and seamless, the new design is even better with absolutely no gaps and no distinct edges.

- More user friendly: The new iOS 8 allows for more natural and fluid swipe gestures, which makes it easier to navigate the phone using only one hand. For instance, navigating Safari or Mail has been made easier, with a simple swipe right to left to go forward, or left to right to go backward.

- Enhanced resolution: An improved resolution means unparalleled brightness, beautiful colors, and flawless images.

Security

Incredible Touch ID technology means the iPhone is more secure than ever before.

- Fingerprint technology: The new password – the fingerprint. Not only can it be used for the password, but also to make purchases on iTunes, iBooks, and the App Store without entering a password.

Apple Pay

The iPhone 6 and 6 Plus can be used as a digital wallet.

- NFC Chip: The new iPhone is equipped with an NFC chip that allows users to pay for purchases at one of the 220,000 contactless payment locations across the US.

- Online payments: Apple Pay also simplifies online payments, allowing users to purchase items with a tap of the Touch ID sensor, which uses the user's fingerprint.

How it works: It will automatically work with the credit card details users have stored in their iTunes account, and it allows users to add more credit cards. Apple has partnered with most US banks, and major credit card providers, meaning this feature will work for virtually everyone.

Faster wireless

With more LTE bands than any other smartphone, and a superfast connection with up to 3x faster Wi-Fi, the iPhone 6 has lighting fast download and upload speeds.

- Wi-Fi calling: Wi-Fi calling allows for convenience when there isn't a good cellular signal available and when abroad. In addition, phones automatically switch over to Voice over LTE when the user steps out of the Wi-Fi range.

Most useful features

of iOS 8

- Goodbye group chat: Sick of that group chat conversation? There is now the option to easily exit the discussion. In addition, there is a "Do Not Disturb" option that allows users to silence the conversation when they need to.

- Quick reply to messages: Previously, users needed to exit what they were working on in order to reply to a new message. Now users are able to swipe down on the message banner that appears and reply to the message without exiting the screen they are on.

- Send multiple pictures in a message: Now clicking on the camera icon on the keyboard when in a message, users will be able to preview up to 20 recent photos, allowing them to select multiple images to send at once.

- Siri can hear you: All the time. Users can simply say "Hey Siri" and no longer need to click on the home button to access her.

- Reply to mail: With a simple swipe to the left. Easy.

- Quick access to apps based on location: At Disney World? A little icon will appear in the lock screen and if the user clicks, they will be brought into the relevant app. This works with many shops and businesses.

Siri and Shazam: One in the same. Siri can recognize songs now, so no need to open the app. Songs can be purchased from the results page.

About 5 mn Smarts

The 5 mn Smarts is a series of short books that help readers gain knowledge of a subject in just 5 minutes with a clear and concise explanation.